Hickory Tree in a Forest

by Frank Coffin
illustrated by Christiane Beauregard

Harcourt
SCHOOL PUBLISHERS

Printed in China

ISBN 10: 0-15-350491-9
ISBN 13: 978-0-15-350491-4

Ordering Options
ISBN 10: 0-15-350333-5 (Grade 3 Below-Level Collection)
ISBN 13: 978-0-15-350333-7 (Grade 3 Below-Level Collection)
ISBN 10: 0-15-357477-1 (package of 5)
ISBN 13: 978-0-15-357477-1 (package of 5)

11 12 13 14 15 0940 12 11 10

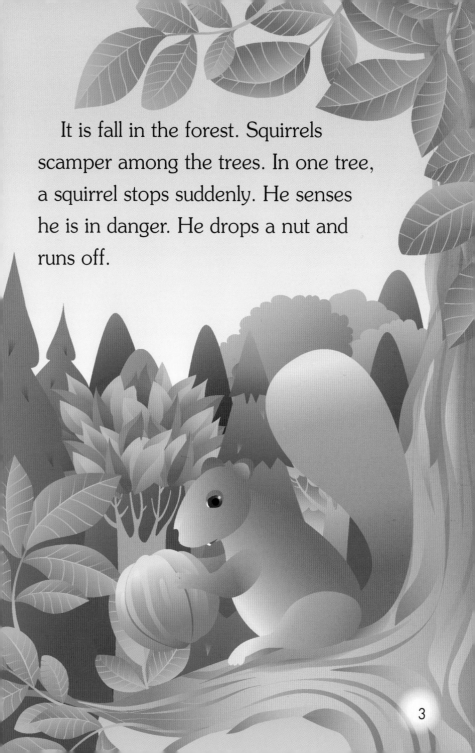

It is fall in the forest. Squirrels scamper among the trees. In one tree, a squirrel stops suddenly. He senses he is in danger. He drops a nut and runs off.

The nut the squirrel dropped falls near other nuts. It strikes a stone and bounces down the ridge. The nut comes to rest near a stream. It lies under the edges of last year's leaves.

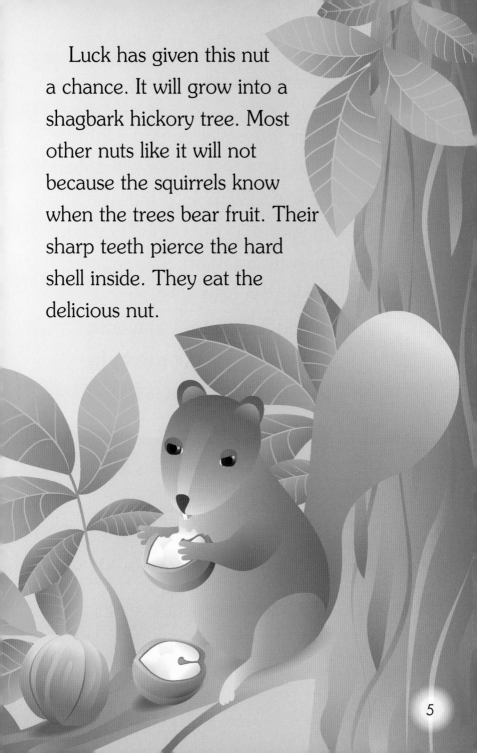

Luck has given this nut a chance. It will grow into a shagbark hickory tree. Most other nuts like it will not because the squirrels know when the trees bear fruit. Their sharp teeth pierce the hard shell inside. They eat the delicious nut.

In some places, you might glimpse a bear under a shagbark hickory. Bears love the sweet meat of hickory nuts. They feast upon them often. The squirrel scolds the bear. The bear is eating the squirrel's favorite food. There is not much the squirrel can do, though!

The hidden nut is not going to be found. During winter, water and time press the nut into the soil. The rabbits and white-footed mice that look for it do not find it.

In April, the seed sprouts. Most of the sprout goes into the ground. The taproot, or main root, of the hickory spears the ground. It is longer than the shoot above the ground.

The hickory keeps growing
slowly in the maze of the forest.
It can grow in the shade. Years
and years pass. The parent tree
keeps dropping nuts, but most
of them never make it this far.
Chipmunks and foxes love to
eat the nuts, too.

After ten years, the tree is about seven feet (2.13 m) tall. It is about as thick as a person's thumb. Its five-leaf leaflets are yellowish green in summer. As fall comes, they turn golden.

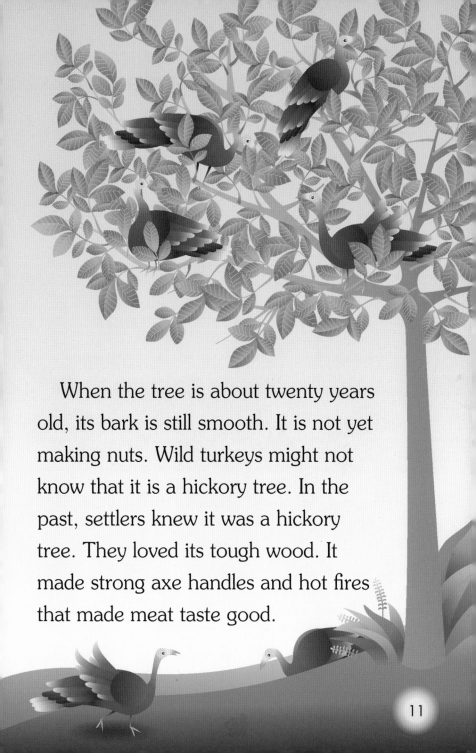

When the tree is about twenty years old, its bark is still smooth. It is not yet making nuts. Wild turkeys might not know that it is a hickory tree. In the past, settlers knew it was a hickory tree. They loved its tough wood. It made strong axe handles and hot fires that made meat taste good.

The hickory faces other dangers besides being chopped down for its wood. Small fires can kill young hickories. Fire damage on large trees can make trees rot. Insects may attack the trees. Birds seeking the insects may make holes in the trees larger.

The smooth bark changes when the tree
is about thirty years old. It begins to split.
Each part of the bark holds tight in the
middle and curves away from the trunk at
the edge. In a few years, the tree takes its
shaggy form.

Nuts begin to appear after about forty years. The tree may live for more than three hundred years. It may reach about eighty feet (24.38 m) in height. It will never be very thick. Bigger beech and maple trees may crowd it out.

This fall, though, animals are happy. Many years ago, they missed a nut while hunting food. Now later generations enjoy the fruit of that mistake.

Think Critically

1. What are some uses of the shagbark hickory tree?

2. What are some dangers hickory trees face?

3. What are some details from this book that interested you?

4. Why do so few hickory nuts grow to become trees?

5. Why do you think the author wrote this book?

 Science

Draw a Diagram Draw four stages of the shagbark hickory tree's life. Write a sentence about each stage below the picture.

School-Home Connection For thousands of years, people have eaten nuts. With family or friends, make a list of kinds of nuts. What are your favorite ways to eat nuts?

Word Count: 524